MIRROR HORSE INTERACTIONS

Copyright Pending

HARNESSING YOUR POWER TO DRIVE FORWARD

The Power to Harness, Hitch, and Drive Your Team to Excellence

A Unique Approach to Team Building

•

Pam Umberger & Cheryl Bess
Mirror Horse Interactions
Wytheville, VA & Somerset, KY
www.mirrorhorse.com
276-228-5817
304-542-1809

•

CAUTION: Equine and carriage driving activities inherently involve risk. Pam Umberger, Cheryl Bess, and Mirror Horse Interactions are not liable for the injury or death of any individual participating in equine and carriage driving activities based on the information in this book.

TABLE OF CONTENTS

Acknowledgements	1
Introduction	3
Harness and Carriage Parts Diagram	5
Parts of the Harness and Carriage – Lesson Material	7
Function and Characteristics	8
Parts of the Harness	10
Parts of the Carriage	13
Activities	15
Discussion Example One – Function Comparisons and Symbolism	15
Name that person or part	
Discussion Example Two – Breast Collar, Neck Strap, Neck Terrets, and Traces	21
Little things make a big difference	
Discussion Example Three – Reins	23
Hold your horses	
Discussion Example Four – Breeching, Hold Back Straps, Hip Straps	25
Don't put the cart before the horse	
Discussion Example Five – The Bit	27
Chomping at the bit	

 Discussion Example Six – Throat Latch   29
  Stop a train wreck before it happens

 Arena Activity One – Group Harnessing   31
  See one, do one

 Arena Activity Two – Group Harnessing as a Team   33
  There is more than one way to shoe a horse

 Arena Activity Three – Be the Horse   35
  Horsin' around

 Arena Activity Four – Ground Driving   37
  Plowing the back forty

 Arena Activity Five – Ground Driving Partnership   39
  There is no "I" in team

 Arena Activity Six – The Power to Harness, Hitch, and Drive Your Team to Excellence   43
  Horse power

Conclusion   45

Appendix A   47
 Horsey Sayings We've All Heard Before

Appendix B   49
 Harness and Carriage Parts Diagram: 1   49
 Harness and Carriage Parts Diagram: 2   50

Appendix C   51
 Order of Harnessing and Unharnessing

ACKNOWLEDGEMENTS

There are so many people to thank for helping us develop this novel approach to Equine Assisted Learning (EAL). Without the events hosted by Sayre Graves at Glenarvon Farm, the idea of working with horse and carriage in an EAL program would not have been possible. We are forever indebted to her for opening an inspirational window.

We wish to express our appreciation to Willie and Debbie Downs for hosting our first EAL event using horse and carriage activities at Crump's Mill Farm. We are thankful for Tom and Ellen Davidson's support of our early endeavors. In the early stages of developing these carriage driving techniques, Mary Jane Umberger of HR Alliance, LLC, gave us the opportunity to prove the effectiveness of the techniques and for that we are grateful. Many thanks to our dear friend Lynn Tuckwiller for proofing and providing a haven to work and write in Florida. Joe LaMay's graphic artistry transformed fragmented pieces into a finished manual. We appreciate Emily Langer's review and contributions. We are indebted to the two local children's homes that participated in carriage driving activities and let us witness these techniques change children's lives. With special thanks to Tim Bess for being "the wind beneath 'her' wings" as Cheryl pursued her dream.

Finally, none of our endeavors could have happened without our dear, kind carriage driving horses. They did and continue to do the most important part of this work.

INTRODUCTION

Fairly early in our work with Equine Assisted Learning, we discovered the close correlation between business relationships and the roles of horse, driver, harness, and carriage. While being involved in the sport of carriage driving, we became aware that many aspects of corporate structures, management dynamics as well as personal and team relationships parallel aspects of carriage driving. For example, the roles of a horse and driver can be comparable to the roles appearing in professional work settings, i.e. workforce and leadership. Likewise, the functions of harness and carriage parts can be compared to various functions of people and teams in business models. Analyzing the characteristics and inter-relatedness of the horse, driver, harness, and carriage can yield profound insights into the nature of professional relationships and the impact on business success.

In this manual, we will show characteristics of harness and carriage parts. We will then demonstrate how to draw on some of the parallels between each specific harness and carriage component and the working parts of a business. Through working with the horse and carriage, clients can become more aware of how they will have a greater chance for success when communication is clear, staff are well-trained, and equipment is in good working order.

Safety is the first and foremost consideration in offering a program including horses and carriage driving. We recommend only experienced and highly-skilled carriage drivers be used as facilitators for this type of program. Every program must provide a safety lecture component for the participants both in basic horse safety and instruction regarding harness and carriage safety. The authors do not accept any responsibility or liability regarding safety or safety instruction while utilizing this approach. Horse handling and carriage driving pose an inherent risk to life and health that must be acknowledged.

Harness and Carriage Parts

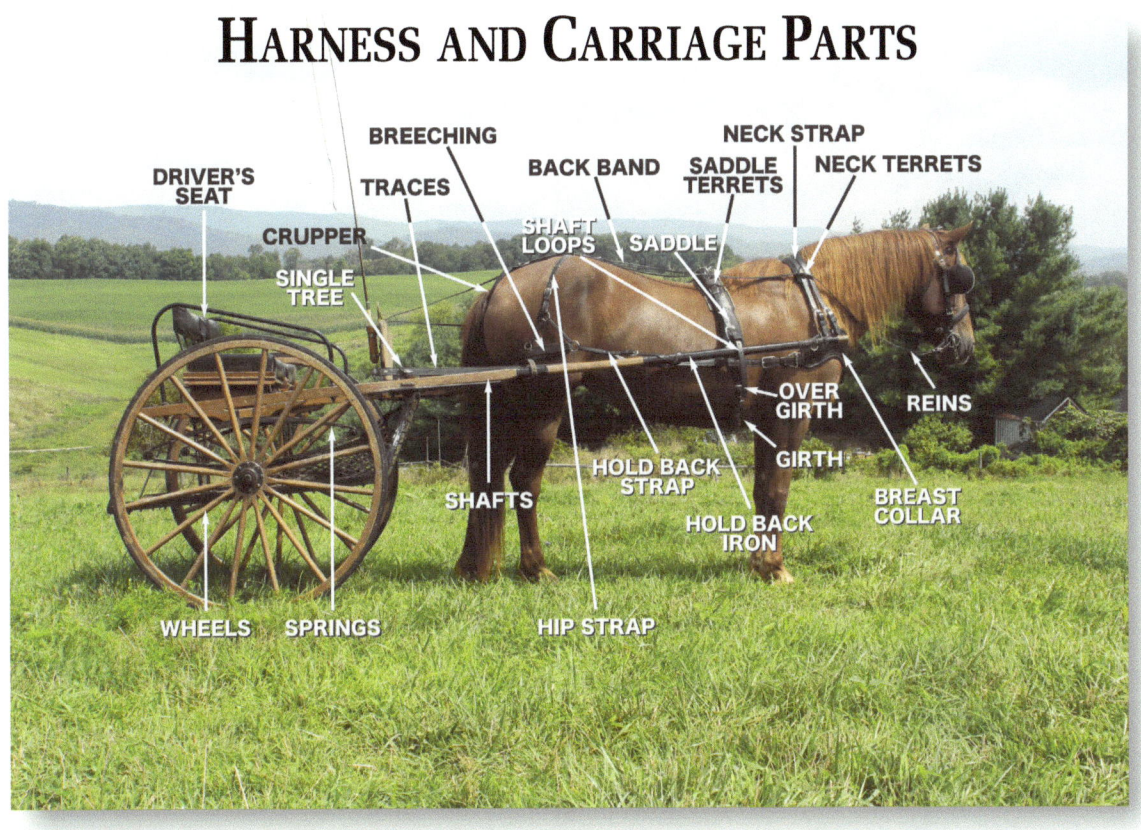

Parts of the Harness and Carriage

Lesson Material

Driving a horse and carriage is a specialty sport which in many aspects differs from other equine activities. Carriage driving shares with other disciplines the importance of having clear and concise communication between horse and human as well as a priority of attention to safety. When riding, the person signals with hands, voice, weight, and legs. In driving, only the hands and voice are used and the driving whip somewhat replaces the legs. As we discuss the function and characteristics of the horse, the driver, and each part of the harness and carriage, we will show how these can represent aspects of people, organizations, or groups.

In the ***Discussion Examples and Arena Activities***, the ***Application Questions*** serve as a guide to comparing the information from the horse activity to the function of the business team. As the discussion develops, facilitators identify additional appropriate questions and guide the group in connecting the principles of the horse activity to the dynamics of the group.

Function & Characteristics of the:

Horse

- Displays power
- Provides source of movement
- Demonstrates strength
- Projects sensitivity
- Reacts to surroundings and behavior of others
- Can be affected by weather, health, fatigue, nutrition
- May or may not understand communication from driver
- May or may not comply with requests of driver
- Demonstrates complex temperament and personality traits

Driver

- Directs
- Controls the horse
- Makes decisions
- Is in charge
- Insures safety
- May or may not display adequate skill and training

Harness

- Exhibits connectedness
- Utilizes power of the horse
- Is complex in function and use
- Has parts that function together as a whole
- Is strong but not cumbersome

Carriage
- Transports driver/passenger/cargo (both function and appearance are relevant.)

PARTS OF THE HARNESS

Breast Collar
- Pushed by horse with its chest

Neck Strap
- Holds breast collar in place
- Is small but essential for safety
- Adjusts for comfort and prevents injury

Neck Terrets
- Keep reins in place, guides for reins
- Serves as guides for reins

Traces
- Transfer forward movement from the breast collar to carriage
- Are attached to carriage at single tree
- Pull the carriage *(horse pushes, traces pull)*

Harness Saddle
- Provides protection, comfort

Saddle Terrets
- Keep reins in place, guides for reins
- Serves as guides for reins

Shaft Loops
- Support cart shafts

Girth
- Stabilizes
- Holds other important parts in place

Overgirth
- Holds shaft loops securely in place and keeps shafts from tipping up

Back Band and Crupper
- Hold proper placement and alignment of other parts

Breeching and Hold Back Straps
- Hold carriage back from running into the rear end of the horse when decreasing speed, stopping, or going downhill

Hip Strap
- Holds breeching in place
- Is small but essential for safety

Bridle Parts

Crown
- Rests on top of horse's head, holds other bridle parts in place

Cheek Straps
- Are an extension of crown, hold bit, support blinders
- Require precise, careful adjustment

Blinders
- Limit horse's field of vision, lessen distractions but may prevent seeing something important
- Require precise, careful adjustment

Cavesson (Noseband)

- May or may not have function, can be used to hold horse's mouth closed

Throat Latch

- Keeps bridle from being rubbed off which would leave the driver without any control of and communication with the horse
- Requires precise, careful adjustment *(If the throat latch is too loose, it is ineffective. If too tight, it can restrict breathing.)*

Bit

- Transmits communication to the horse to turn, slow down, stop, or back up
- Requires correct adjustment, type, and size for comfort and effectiveness
- Varies with preference of each individual horse and can be considered mild, strong, or harsh in nature

Reins

- Convey communication
- Are the only physical connectionbetween driver and horse
- Need to be comfortable in width and thickness for each individual driver

Parts of the Carriage

Shafts
- Support and guide the carriage

Hold Back Irons
- Keep hold back straps from sliding on shafts

Single Tree
- Is the point of attachment for traces to pull carriage, reduces friction and stress on horse's shoulders

Springs
- Provide comfort, cushion bumps

Wheels
- Roll when horse moves forward or backward

Seat
- Provides comfort and support for driver

Fifth Wheel
- Allows a 4-wheel carriage to turn smoothly

Brake
- Enables the driver to help control momentum and burden on horse downhill

ACTIVITIES

Note: In the **Discussion Examples and Arena Activities**, the **Application Questions** serve as a guide to comparing the information from the horse activity to the function of the business team. As the discussion develops, facilitators identify additional appropriate questions and guide the group in connecting the principles of the horse activity to the dynamics of the group.

Discussion Example One

FUNCTION COMPARISONS AND SYMBOLISM
Name that Person or Part

HORSE: The horse is the source of strength and is the power that provides movement. It can move at a variety of speeds as well as stand still. Ideally, there is clear communication between horse and driver and the horse goes according to the direction of the driver. The horse is specifically trained for this job over months or years to build confidence and competence.

APPLICATION: Participants will determine and discuss who or what functions as the horse in their work setting.

DRIVER: The driver is the person in charge and makes the decisions regarding direction and speed of travel. The driver needs to communicate clearly to the horse and be fair and reasonable with requests based on reactions from the horse. When making decisions, the driver takes into consideration the fitness, training, and experience of the horse, and is responsible for horse safety, and others in surrounding area.

APPLICATION: Participants will determine and discuss who or what functions as the driver in their work setting.

HARNESS: The function and purpose of the harness parts can be compared to corporate and team structures.

APPLICATION: Participants will review description of harness parts and compare them with people, job positions, departments, or objects that function in a similar manner within their business or work setting.

Breast Collar
- Transmits power, is point of contact for forward movement

Neck Strap
- Acts as side support, prevents misplacement, and is small but essential for safety

Neck Terrets
- Provide guidance, act as a pathway

Traces
- Transmit power causing movement and connect power and purpose

Harness Saddle
- Provides protection and comfort

Saddle Terrets
- Provide guidance, act as a pathway

Shaft Loops
- Support, hold up

Girth
- Provides stability and connects necessary parts, is adjustable

Overgirth
- Stabilizes, holds down

Back Band and Crupper
- Hold together, offer central stability

Breeching and Hold Back Straps
- Control excessive forward movement, avoid moving foward too rapidly, avoid interference, and prevent purpose from clashing with power

Hip Strap
- Is necessary for support and stability
- Holds proper function in place
- Ensures safety

Bridle Parts
Communication, control, interconnectedness, focus

Crown
- Supports, establishes interconnectedness

Cheek Straps
- Provide support, interconnectedness, and can be adjusted

Blinders
- Aid focus, eliminate distractions, limit visual input

Cavesson (Noseband)
- Restricts mouth movement

Throat Latch
- Prevents dangerous displacement and loss of control
- Is small but essential for safety *(If too loose, it is ineffective and can lead to dangerous loss. If too tight, can smother, choke, or cut off air.)*

Bit
- Facilitates communication as well as control of direction, speed, and intensity

Reins
- Control pace and direction of decision making
- Provide direct line of communication and negotiation
- Create balance between mental and physical strength
- Offer variable level of connection depending on amount of contact

CARRIAGE: The function and purpose of the carriage parts can be compared to corporate and team structures.

APPLICATION: Participants will review description of carriage parts and compare them with people, job positions, departments, or objects that function in a similar manner within their business and work setting.

Shafts:
- Stabilize, connect, guide, restrict

Hold Back Irons:
- Prevent displacement, are small but important parts

Single Tree:
- Frees movement, reduces friction, connects power and purpose

Springs:
- Promote comfort, absorb energy

Seat:
- Provides comfort and support

Wheels:
- Facilitate movement

Fifth Wheel:
- Allows more efficient changes of direction

Brake:
- Decreases speed and work load

Discussion Example Two

BREAST COLLAR, NECK STRAP, NECK TERRETS, TRACES

Little things make a big difference

Function of Harness Parts on the Horse:

Breast Collar:
- Pushed by horse with its chest

Neck Strap:
- Holds breast collar in place
- Is small but essential for safety
- Adjusts for comfort and prevents injury

Neck Terrets:
- Keep reins in place, guides for reins
- Serves as guides for reins

Traces:
- Transfer forward movement from breast collar to carriage
- Are attached to carriage at single tree
- Pull the carriage *(horse pushes, traces pull)*

Symbolism of Harness Parts:

Breast Collar:
- Transmits power, is point of contact for forward movement

Neck Strap:
- Acts as side support, prevents misplacement, and is small but essential for safety

Neck Terrets:
- Provide guidance, act as pathway

Traces:
- Transmit power causing movement and connect power and purpose

APPLICATION:
- *Who or what functions as the breast collar? (Works with source of strength and power to create movement)*
- *Who or what functions as the neck strap? (Supportive, holds and connects, small but essential)*
- *Who or what functions as the neck terrets? (Helps keep communication in place)*
- *Who or what functions as the traces? (Transfers energy and movement from the power source to the group)*

Discussion Example Three

REINS

Hold your horses

Function of Harness Parts on the Horse:
- Reins are the only direct line of communication between driver and horse. Driver training and skill are key elements to clear communication with the horse. The driver's hands transmit information by pulling or releasing one rein or the other and by pulling or releasing both reins together. Through the reins, the driver communicates firmness, gentleness, smoothness, or harshness.

Symbolism of Reins:
- Control pace and direction of decision making
- Provide direct line of communication and negotiation
- Create balance between mental and physical strength
- Offer variable level of connection depending on amount of contact

APPLICATION:
- *Who or what functions as the reins in your organization?*
- *What type of reins exist in your organization?*
- *Is communication in your organization clear, timely, adequate, consistent, and purposeful?*

Discussion Example Four

BREECHING, HOLD BACK STRAPS, HIP STRAPS

Don't put the cart before the horse

Function of Harness Parts on the Horse:
Breeching and hold back straps:
- Hold carriage back from running into the rear end of the horse when decreasing speed, stopping, or going down hill

Hip strap:
- Holds breeching in place
- Is small but essential for safety

Symbolism of Harness Parts:
Breeching and hold back straps:
- Control excessive forward movement, avoid moving forward too rapidly, avoid interference, and prevent purpose from clashing with power

Hip strap:
- Is necessary for support and stability
- Holds proper function in place
- Ensures safety

APPLICATION:
- *Who in your organization holds back or stops __undesired__ or unnecessary forward movement?*

- *Who in your organization holds back or stops **desired** or necessary forward movement?*
- *Who or what keeps speed of movement safe and reasonable?*
- *Who or what keeps the purpose and source of power from colliding?*
- *Who or what keeps things in their proper place and is supportive?*

Discussion Example Five

THE BIT

Chomping at the bit

Function of the Bit on the Horse:
- Transmits communication to the horse to turn, slow down, stop, or back up
- Requires correct adjustment, type, and size for comfort and effectiveness
- Varies with preference of each individual horse and can be considered mild, strong, or harsh in nature

Symbolism of the Bit:
- Facilitates communication as well as control of direction, speed, and intensity

APPLICATION:
- *Who or what serves as a communicator in your organization?*
- *What does communication look like in your organization? (Mild/Strong/Harsh)*
- *When communication is delivered in your organization, what does the usual response look like?*
- *Have the participants decide, as a group, the bit that best symbolizes communication mechanisms in their organization. [NOTE: Have a box of bits available for hands-on demonstration.]*

Discussion Example Six

THROAT LATCH

Stop a train wreck before it happens

Function of the Throat Latch on the Horse:
- Keeps the bridle from being rubbed off which would leave the driver without any control of and communication with the horse
- Requires precise, careful adjustment *(If the throat latch is too loose, it is ineffective. If too tight, it can restrict breathing.)*

Symbolism of the Throat Latch:
- Prevents dangerous displacement and loss of control
- Is small but essential for safety
  (If too loose, it is ineffective and can lead to dangerous loss. If too tight, can smother, choke, or cut off air.)

APPLICATION:
- *Who or what keeps the components of communication and control in place and working in your organization?*
- *What happens in your organization if safety procedures are too lax or not functioning?*
- *What happens in your organization if control is too tight and performance is stifled or choked?*

Arena Activity One

GROUP HARNESSING

See one, do one

Description:

Assemble participants in arena. Have the horse handler manage the horse with a lead rope at all times.

OPTION ONE: The most challenging exercise is to have the facilitators direct the participants to harness the horse without any instruction or demonstration.

OPTION TWO: The least challenging option is to have the facilitators quickly harness the horse and verbally identify all harness parts with description of function. Facilitators then remove the harness and place it off to the side.

Without further instruction, the participants are instructed to harness the horse. The facilitators leave the arena and observe from the sidelines. Participants are to indicate to the horse handler when they have completed the task. At this time, the horse handler and facilitators are NOT to answer questions regarding the process of harnessing the horse. Allow 15 minutes for this part of the exercise.

For the next stage of this exercise, participants remain in the arena. Horse is unharnessed. Participants are given a diagram of a harnessed horse with parts labeled and directions for harnessing the horse *(see Appendices B and C.)* Facilitators again demonstrate how to harness the horse properly. Facilitators remove the harness and instruct participants to harness the horse. This time, the participants are allowed to ask questions and receive instruction from the facilitators.

APPLICATION:

- *Describe your experience with harnessing the horse.*
- *Were you able to accomplish the task the first time?*
- *Initially, what was the most difficult part of harnessing the horse?*
- *What did you notice about the horse during your first attempt to harness?*
- *What did you notice about the horse when you had guidance and could request assistance?*
- *Did you notice any difference in your performance when you had a diagram with parts labeled, received another demonstration, had guidance, and could request instruction?*
- *Did the group work together well? If not, when did you encounter difficulty?*
- *Are there parts of this exercise that parallel situations in your work setting?*

Arena Activity Two

GROUP HARNESSING AS A TEAM

There is more than one way to shoe a horse

Description:

Participants are instructed to work as a team to harness the horse. They should have received instruction and have very basic knowledge of this process. Participants are to have a 5-minute planning period. *(The facilitators can have the participants perform any or all of the options below.)*

Option 1:

- All participants can make decisions, talk, and give directions as the harness is placed on the horse.

Option 2:
- The group identifies a team leader. As a group, participants place the harness on the horse.
ONLY the team leader can speak and give instructions. Team members can only do what is instructed.

Option 3:
- The group identifies a team leader. As a group, participants place the harness on the horse. The team leader guides the process and communicates with the team members. Team members can verbally communicate with each other and the team leader.

APPLICATION:
- *Which method did you find provided the desired outcome of properly and efficiently harnessing the horse?*
- *What did you discuss during your 5-minute planning session?*
- *If you picked a team leader, how was it done?*
- *What did you find to be the most challenging part of this exercise?*
- *Did you function as a team? How were decisions made?*
- *When harnessing, did you take the horse into consideration?*
- *What response(s) did you receive from the horse? What caused that response?*
- *Compare and contrast communication patterns in this exercise to communication patterns in your work setting.*

Arena Activity Three

BE THE HORSE

Horsin' around

Description:

Participants will divide into pairs. Each pair will be given a set of reins and a blindfold. One person will perform as the "horse." The "horse" will be blindfolded and hold the end of a rein in each hand. The other person will stand behind the "horse," hold the reins and will "drive" the "horse" through a simple obstacle course. The "driver" can only use the words "get up" and "whoa." The "horse" can only communicate through horse-like body language and sounds – no words. The pair will switch roles and repeat the activity through the obstacle course.

This activity demonstrates how much trust the horse must have and how easy it is to get confused. It also demonstrates how hard it is to give clear direction, especially in a distracting environment.

APPLICATION:

- *Describe your experience functioning as the "horse."*
- *Describe your experience functioning as the "driver."*
- *Did communication go both ways or was it one-sided? Was it consistent?*
- *Was there communication other than through the reins?*
- *Can you relate this experience to your workplace?*

(Thank you, Emily Langer, for sharing this exercise.)

Arena Activity Four

GROUND DRIVING

Plowing the back forty

Description:
Ground driving can be done with a driving bridle, harness, and driving reins on the horse. It can also be done quite simply with driving reins attached to the side of a horse's halter and using a training surcingle to keep the reins in place. *(The most important determination on whether to use a bridle and bit or a halter is based on whether you as the facilitator believe the participants can both safely and*

compassionately use the reins with a bit in the horse's mouth.)

After basic instruction and demonstration by the facilitator in the use of rein control and signals to communicate with the horse, the participants will ground drive the horse with the reins. Safety will remain the priority during this and all exercises. The participants will learn and demonstrate how to ask the horse to walk forward, turn left, turn right, and stop by navigating a simple obstacle course. (The horse handler or facilitator may initially assist by having a lead rope on the horse.)

APPLICATION:
- *What did you notice about the horse's behavior?*
- *Did you feel connected to the horse?*
- *What did you notice about the lines of communication with the horse?*
- *Did you utilize anything other than the reins to communicate with the horse?*
- *Did the communication go both ways in this exercise or was it one-sided?*
- *What did you notice about your communication style while interacting with the horse?*
- *Compare and contrast communication patterns in this exercise to communication patterns in you work setting.*

Arena Activity Five

GROUND DRIVING PARTNERSHIP

There is no "I" in team

Description:

Participants are asked to work in groups of two. The arena has one or more obstacle courses built with cones, poles, and barrels, etc. The horse or horses are prepared to ground drive and can either be in full harness or in halter, training surcingle, and reins. *(The most important determination on whether to use a bridle and bit or a halter is based on whether you as the facilitator believe the participants can both safely and compassionately use the reins with a bit in the horse's mouth.)*

Option 1:

Each pair will then be asked to ground drive a horse through the obstacle course. You may choose to have each participant drive the course up and back OR the first participant will drive one way and switch to the other partner to return. One member of each pair may assist his or her partner at anytime. Each obstacle course should have a facilitator and horse handler available at all times.

Option 2:

Prior to dividing into pairs, the facilitators can have the participants divide into two teams to build their own obstacle courses without prior knowledge of their purpose.

Option 3:

Each pair of participants is asked to ground drive the horse simultaneously with one person managing the left rein and the other person managing the right rein. (They may be asked to remain connected by locking arms, holding hands, or holding a short rope.)

APPLICATION:
- *What did you notice about the horse's response and willingness to navigate the obstacle course?*

- *What did you notice about your response to navigating an obstacle course while ground driving a horse?*
- *How did you communicate with your partner?*
- *How did you communicate with the horse?*
- *What was the most challenging part of this exercise?*
- *Was it easier to ground drive the horse individually or combined with your partner?*
- *How did the horse respond to two drivers?*
- *Did this exercise become a competition?*
- *Compare and contrast communication patterns in this exercise to communication patterns in your work setting.*

42

Arena Activity Six

THE POWER TO HARNESS, HITCH, AND DRIVE YOUR TEAM TO EXCELLENCE

Horse Power

Description:

The participants will be asked to harness a horse with the direct guidance and observation of the facilitators. The facilitators will hitch the horse to the carriage while providing detailed explanation of the process and safety measures.
The facilitators will then drive the horse and demonstrate the function of parts previously identified in the learning section of this book.

Each participant will be given a chance to ride in the carriage with the facilitator. They will directly observe how the horse, driver, harness, and carriage work together to successfully move in all directions. Based on the observed skill level and desire of the participant, the participant will drive the carriage around the arena with the facilitator in the carriage. At least two horse handlers should be available for this part of the activity.

APPLICATION:

- *What did you notice about communication and safety during harnessing and hitching the horse?*
- *What did you notice about the horse's reaction to being hitched to the carriage?*
- *What components did it take to move forward in a horse drawn carriage both physically and strategically?*
- *Can you compare the skills used in driving a horse and carriage to a project or process within your organization?*
- *Compare and contrast communication patterns in this exercise to communication patterns in your work setting.*

Conclusion

The results at the completion of a carriage driving program can have various outcomes. Remain open to outcomes with the horse and carriage providing the driving force. Doing so ensures your participants gain valuable insights into their team dynamics. It inspires the participants to think outside the box, find success in everyday work situations, and reach future goals.

This program is intended to provide the framework for an intense and thought-providing day of learning, critical thinking, self-exploration, and problem-solving. The profound insights gained from these activities can launch a team forward to find and **"harness their horse power"**. It is time to step up to Equine Assisted Learning and carriage driving.

- Appendix A -
Horsey Sayings We've All Heard Before

You can lead a horse to water but you can't make him drink
Horsin' around
Stubborn as a mule
Got the bit between his teeth
Chomping at the bit
Ridden hard and put up wet
In a lather
Horse sense
Don't put the cart before the horse
Rein him/her in
That's a horse of a different color
He or she is the kingpin
Horsepower
Circle the wagons
Dark horse
Don't look a gift horse in the mouth
Don't shut the stable door after the horse has bolted
Get off your high horse
Beating a dead horse
Hold your horses
Horse feathers
If wishes were horses beggars would ride
Pony up
Straight from the horses mouth
Make hay while the sun shines

- Appendix B -
Harness & Carriage Parts Diagram: 1

- Appendix B -
Harness & Carriage Parts Diagram: 2

- Appendix C -
Order of Harnessing and Unharnessing

Harnessing a Horse
1. Slip neck strap over horse's head and breast collar to horse's chest.
2. Put harness saddle on back, hip strap over hip, & breeching around rear.
3. Buckle girth, then over girth (loosely), then crupper.
4. Put on bridle, then run reins through back terret, neck terret, and attach to bit.

Unharnessing a Horse
1. Unbuckle reins from bit. Remove bridle. Put on halter.
2. Either remove reins from harness OR put rein ends in saddle terrets and run long part of reins through left saddle terret.
3. Unbuckle crupper, then over girth, then girth.
4. Remove harness saddle, hip strap, etc. all together.
5. Remove breast collar by slipping neck strap over horse's head.

The End

NOTES

NOTES

www.ingramcontent.com/pod-product-compliance
Lightning Source LLC
Chambersburg PA
CBHW050751110526
44592CB00002B/31